EXTINCT INSECTS

and those in danger of extinction

Philip Steele

Franklin Watts
New York London Toronto Sydney

First published in the United States
by Franklin Watts
387 Park Avenue South
New York, N.Y. 10016

Consultant: Professor Richard T. J. Moody,
BSc, Dip Ed, PhD, FGS.
Design: Julian Holland Publishing Ltd
Picture researcher: Jennifer Johnson
Illustrator: Cecilia Fitzsimons
Cartography: Gecko Ltd

Printed in the United Kingdom

Library of Congress Cataloging-in-Publication Data

Steele, Philip.
    Extinct insects/Philip Steele.
        p.   cm.
    Includes index
    Summary: Discusses the physical
characteristics of several endangered,
extinct, and prehistoric species of
insects.
    ISBN 0-531-11032-X
    1. Insects, Fossil – Juvenile literature.
[1. Insects. 2. Insects, Fossil. 3. Extinct
animals.] I. Title.
QE831.S74 1991   90-45890
565'.7-dc20   CIP AC

Picture acknowledgements:
pp5 C W Helliwell/Oxford Scientific
Films, 8 Natural Science Photos, 9 Frieder
Sauer/Bruce Coleman Ltd, 16 Robert
Goodden/Worldwide Butterflies Ltd,
17 Worldwide Butterflies Ltd, 20 J Fennell/
Bruce Coleman Ltd, 21 Joe Dorsey/ Oxford
Scientific Films, 22 Michael Fogden/
Oxford Scientific Films, 25 Kim Taylor/
Bruce Coleman Ltd, 26 Kjell Sandved/
Oxford Scientific Films, 27 New Forest
Butterfly Farm, Ashurst.

Contents

Large coppers

Brilliant coppery wings marked with black make the large copper butterfly one of the more beautiful types, or species, of insect found in Europe and Asia. In the last century this splendid butterfly was often killed and mounted by butterfly hunters for their collections.

Butterfly collectors may have played their part in making the large copper extinct, but the main cause was the draining of wetlands. The large copper needed wet ditches in order to breed. During the 1840s it was found that the large copper was becoming scarcer and scarcer in the British Isles. By 1865 the butterfly was extinct in Britain.

Since the last century, more and more insect species have been threatened with extinction. Recent extinctions of moths and butterflies have been reported from Hawaii, South Africa, the islands of Mauritius and the Seychelles, and Taiwan in Asia.

1840 Large copper butterfly became scarce in Britain.
1865 Large copper extinct in Britain.

▼ Copper butterflies are under threat around the world. Two threatened species, the Hermes copper and Clayton's copper, are found in the United States, where changes to their habitat and over-collection by butterfly hunters have seriously reduced numbers.

Clayton's copper

THE SURVIVORS
- Large coppers still exist in some parts of the world, but the British large copper was recognized by scientists as a separate kind, or race.
- In 1927, a Dutch race of the large copper was introduced in Cambridgeshire, England. It has survived, but only with careful protection and land management. It has not managed to spread to other sites.

▲ The large copper has a wingspan of about 40 mm (1.5 in). The female has wings that are spotted and edged in black. The male has only two black spots on its forewings. The insect feeds on the great water dock, a plant of the wetlands.

One million species

The world has not always been the same. Over the ages, it has gone through many gradual changes. The land masses and the seas have changed position. The climate has at times been much colder than it is today, and at times, much warmer. Plants and animals have adapted to the changing conditions or have become extinct. New kinds of creatures have evolved to take their place.

The age of insects began over 400 million years ago. These creatures were among the most successful new forms of life on Earth, and today they make up at least 80 percent of all known animal species. There are about one million insect species on record, but there may be six times as many that have not been discovered yet.

Insects live in soil, air or water. Some insects can breed at an amazing rate. In theory, a single pair of cabbage aphids could have 1,560,000,000,000,000,000,000,000 descendants in a single season. In fact, vast numbers of them are eaten by other insects.

► The largest insect known lived between 310 and 290 million years ago. It was named *Meganeura monyi*. Although it looked very much like today's dragonflies, it was much bigger and had a wingspan of about 90 cm (35 in).

Meganeura monyi larvae lived in the shallow water of the swamps which then covered the earth. Adults hunted on the wing, feeding on the smaller insects that swarmed over the rotting plants and in the murky waters.

▼ The life cycle of a butterfly has four stages. The life cycle of a grasshopper has three.

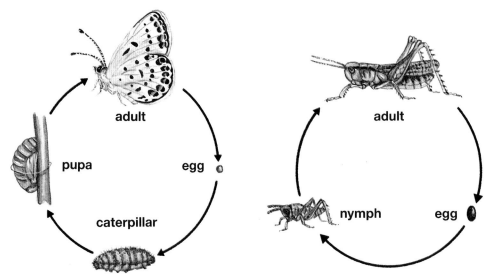

adult

pupa   egg

caterpillar

adult

nymph   egg

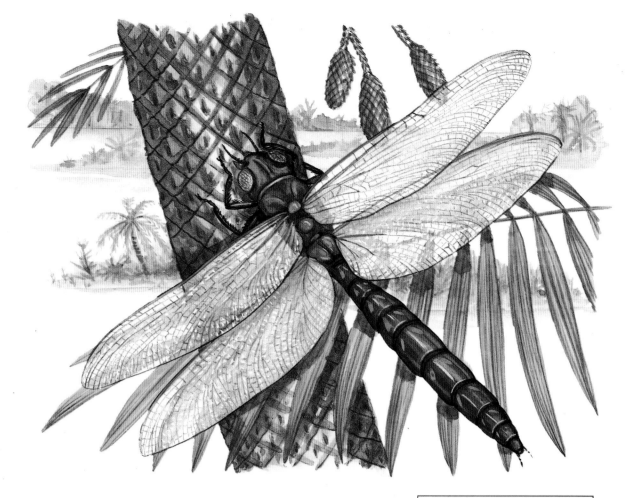

What is an insect?

Insects are small, boneless creatures whose bodies are covered in a tough, hard casing. An insect has six legs and its body is divided into three parts – head, thorax and abdomen. Most insects can fly, and have one or two pairs of wings.

Insects go through various stages during their lives. Some insects, like butterflies, have a four-stage life cycle. They start life as an egg, which hatches into a larva or caterpillar. This turns into a pupa before becoming an adult.

Other insects, like grasshoppers, have three stages in their life cycle. The egg hatches into a nymph, which looks like the adult but does not have wings. Finally the nymph becomes an adult.

420-400 million years ago: The first insects evolved.
310 million years ago: *Meganeura* hunted the swamps.
290 million years ago: *Meganeura* became extinct.

Clues to the past

Insects do not have big bones. Small insect bodies are easily crushed and scattered, and are often eaten by other animals. Even so, traces of extinct insects and other tiny creatures can still be found. They are mostly impressions, often of wings, pressed into mud or volcanic ash long ago. Over millions of years the mud and ash have turned into hard rock. The marks left behind are called fossils.

Where no insect fossils survive, it is still clear that insects existed because of the plant fossils that have been found. Many plants need insects to survive. The insects carry the plants' pollen with them when they go from plant to plant looking for nectar. Some flowering plants need pollen from another plant before they can bear seeds and fruit. By studying which type of plant needs which type of insect to pollinate it, scientists can work out the type of insect that would have lived around a particular plant.

◀ Amber is a yellowish brown, clear substance formed from the fossilized resin of ancient fir trees. Many insects are preserved in amber. Long ago, insects were trapped in the sticky resin, which then hardened in the air. This bee died about 100,000 million years ago, and yet every detail of its shape can still be seen.

▲ This dragonfly lived millions of years ago. The marks of its wings have been preserved in rock as a fossil.

Island species

Insect species that are most at risk are those found only in a very small area. Since they have adapted to a very localized habitat, they are in danger if that habitat is disturbed. Many extinct species lived on islands, and many of the species that are threatened today are also island-dwellers. These insects are often unable to move to another habitat if their own is threatened by people clearing the land or by a natural disaster.

1850 Lord Howe Island well populated with stick insects.
1918 Black rats arrived on Lord Howe Island.
1980 Lord Howe Island stick insects probably extinct.

◀ Lord Howe Island lies nearly 700 km (435 mi) northeast of Sydney, Australia. It is only 13 sq km (5 sq mi) in area, with forested hills and open grassland. One hundred years ago, the island was teeming with a species of stick insect, 12 cm (5 in) long and colored reddish brown to black.

In 1918 black rats from a wrecked ship swam onto the island and ate the insects. Some may have survived on a nearby island, but this unusual-looking species of stick insect now seems to be extinct.

The giant earwig

The biggest species of earwig in the world lives on the lonely island of St. Helena, in the middle of the South Atlantic Ocean. These earwigs are found only in the northeast of the island, on Horse Point Plain.

The St. Helena earwig seems to be disappearing, but scientists do not know why. To carry out a detailed survey of one insect species is expensive and takes a lot of time. So many insects are threatened that scientists cannot keep up with all the research work that is necessary. Without more information about the St. Helena earwig, its future, like that of many other insects, is uncertain.

▼ The St. Helena earwig has reddish legs and a black body which can measure up to 90 mm (3.5 in) long. It lives under boulders and in tussocks of grass.

Hawaiian disaster

The Hawaiian Islands lie in the middle of the Pacific Ocean. When the English sailor and explorer Captain James Cook visited the islands in 1778, he found white sands, blue seas and lush, green forests. Today, many of the forests have been cleared and buildings put up in their place. Three thousand species of plants brought in from other lands now grow on the islands, and over 270 of the islands' own native plant species have disappeared altogether. Many insects depended on these native plants for their survival. At least one-third of the islands' insect species have become extinct.

Fruit flies

About 500 species of fruit flies are known to have developed, or evolved, in the Hawaiian Islands. Today, they are found mostly in the highland forests. However, these forests are being cleared so that the land can be used for grazing cattle and growing crops such as sugar cane and pineapples. The fruit flies are being killed by pesticides and eaten by other insects brought to the islands from elsewhere.

▶ Some insects have adapted to the native vegetation of the Hawaiian Islands. Within national parks, the insects' habitats have been protected, but elsewhere changes have been disastrous. Many species cannot survive on plants that have been introduced to the region.

DID YOU KNOW?
- The Hawaiian island of Oahu has 27 species of insect that are found nowhere else on Earth.
- Recent extinctions on the Hawaiian Islands include 4 weevil species, 7 moth species, and 2 fly species.
- Hawaiian species in danger today include 12 moths, 12 damselflies, 1 fly, 9 weevils, 12 wasps, 1 bee, 6 crickets, and 14 beetles.

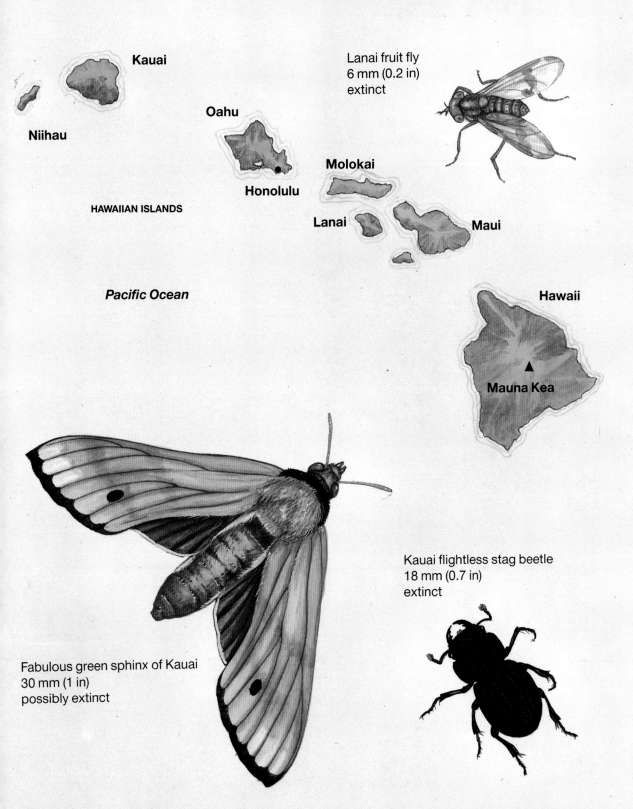

Kauai

Niihau

Oahu

Honolulu

HAWAIIAN ISLANDS

Molokai

Lanai

Maui

Lanai fruit fly
6 mm (0.2 in)
extinct

Pacific Ocean

Hawaii

Mauna Kea

Kauai flightless stag beetle
18 mm (0.7 in)
extinct

Fabulous green sphinx of Kauai
30 mm (1 in)
possibly extinct

The blues

There is a family of butterflies found in most parts of the world which scientists call Lycaenids, but they are most often known as blues, coppers, or hairstreaks.

Today, 78 species of these butterflies are threatened in one way or another. The Lycaenids are at risk because many have a very small breeding range. Whole populations can be destroyed if bad weather or some other natural disaster affects their habitat or food supply.

The large blue was affected by changes to the countryside where it lived. This species of butterfly was always rare in Britain. Then, early this century, some of the grassy hillsides where it lived were plowed up for crops. On other hillsides in its range, many of the rabbits which nibbled the grass died of myxomatosis. The grass grew longer and longer and became overgrown. The result was that the red ant could no longer nest there. The red ant plays a vital role in the life cycle of the large blue. By 1979, the butterfly was extinct in Britain.

Late 18th century: Large blue recorded in Britain.
1950s Rabbits died of myxomatosis.
1975 Large blue protected by British law.
1979 Large blue probably became extinct in Britain.

DID YOU KNOW?
- The large blue butterfly was discovered in Britain in 1795 and had a wingspan of 38 mm (1.5 in).
- The dwarf blue butterfly of South Africa is the world's smallest butterfly, with a wingspan of only 14 mm (0.6 in).
- The blues and coppers are often found on open grassy areas where there are many wild flowers, while the hairstreaks tend to live in woodlands.

▲ The Palos Verdes blue butterfly of the United States may have become extinct as a result of an unseasonal snow storm.

Red ants and blue butterflies

The female large blue lays her eggs on wild thyme in the summer. The eggs hatch into caterpillars which feed on the flowers of the thyme plant.

The caterpillars drop off the plant and are carried into the nests of red ants. The red ants "milk" the caterpillars for a sweet liquid which is given out near the tail. In return, the caterpillar is allowed to feed on the grubs and eggs of the ants.

The adult butterfly escapes from the ants' nest the following summer and breeds again.

▼ The large blue depends on another creature, the red ant, for its survival. This means that it faces a double risk. If the habitat of the red ant is disturbed, this can be as much of a threat to the butterfly as the disturbance of its own habitat and food plants.

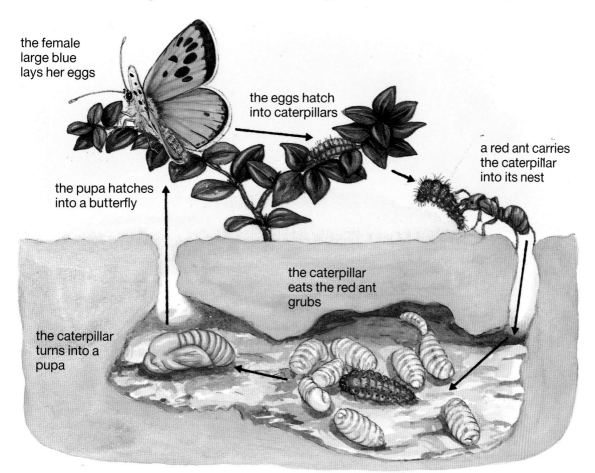

the female large blue lays her eggs

the eggs hatch into caterpillars

a red ant carries the caterpillar into its nest

the pupa hatches into a butterfly

the caterpillar eats the red ant grubs

the caterpillar turns into a pupa

At risk

Bird-winged butterflies

Bird-winged butterflies live in Australasia and New Guinea. They are the most impressive of all butterflies, with huge flapping wings.

Eight bird-winged species are at risk of becoming extinct, including the splendid paradise bird-winged. The forests where the endangered species live have been cleared so that crops can be planted.

In the past, the butterflies were also hunted by collectors. However, since 1966, the bird-winged butterfly has been protected by law. Other bird-winged species are rare and are found only within a very limited range.

◀ The Queen Alexandra bird-winged butterfly is found only on the Popondetta Plain in Northern Province, Papua New Guinea. The male has green and blue wings that are narrower and rounder than those of the larger female. The female is brown with creamy markings.

The Queen Alexandra bird-winged is listed by the International Union for the Conservation of Nature and Natural Resources (IUCN) as an endangered species because its forest habitat is being cut down.

Swallowtails

Swallowtails are found in Asia, North Africa, Europe and in parts of North America. This species of butterfly is in decline in parts of Central Europe and also in England. The English swallowtails are fussy feeders. Their caterpillars will eat only milk parsley, a wetland weed. In many places their habitat has been destroyed as marshes have been drained for farming, and in some places the milk parsley plants have become overgrown.

DID YOU KNOW?
- The bird-winged butterflies are part of a large family of butterflies that includes the swallowtails. Nearly 90 members of the family are at risk.
- The Queen Alexandra butterfly is the world's largest and heaviest butterfly. It has a wingspan of 280 mm (11 in) and weighs over 25 g (0.9 oz).

▼ The African giant swallowtail lives in the rain forests of West and Central Africa. This rare butterfly is almost as large as the bird-winged butterflies, with a wingspan of over 260 mm (10 in). Its body is very poisonous and its black and orange markings serve as a warning to birds and mammals.

Damsels and dragons

Damselflies and the large dragonflies are some of the most beautiful insects alive today. They have shimmering wings and bodies colored in metallic blues and greens. They feed on other insects, which they catch in midair. They lay their eggs in fresh water, and the young, or nymphs, spend their early life underwater.

The main threat to dragonflies comes from the drainage of wetland. Mechanical diggers scoop out deep ditches, destroying plant and insect life. Water levels in the lakes and rivers are often raised or lowered with pumps. This disturbs the habitat of the dragonflies. Insecticides, weed-killers and fertilizers have poisoned both land and water for many dragonfly species. Conifer forests have been planted, and these often overshadow the edges of ponds and lakesides where dragonflies and damselflies would usually live and feed.

▼ Until 1978, scientists thought that the black San Francisco forktail was extinct. It is now thought to have survived against all the odds. It is found along the California coast between Point Reyes and Monterey. This species of damselfly has suffered because its habitat has been built over, dredged and polluted. The protected site where it may survive is along the Point Reyes National Seashore.

▲ The rare shining macromia dragonfly has a black and yellow body with a bronzelike sheen. It is found in south-western France between the Dordogne River and the Golfe du Lion. The streams near which it lives have become polluted or have been channeled through pipes by farmers. These changes to the dragonfly's habitat mean that its future is threatened.

DID YOU KNOW?
- Over 130 species of dragonfly and damselfly are at risk around the world today.
- Damselflies fly relatively slowly, and are often eaten by the larger and faster dragonflies.

Flightless crickets

Before Polynesian islanders settled in New Zealand nearly 1,000 years ago, the wildlife of the islands had few enemies. As a result, many birds and insects lost the power of flight.

Wetas are wingless crickets which live in trees and caves. Today their habitat is threatened, and without wings they cannot fly away to find a more suitable place to live.

The giant wetas have been killed by cats and rats in New Zealand. These were introduced when ships from Europe visited the islands. The destruction of the countryside for building has also caused the death of many wetas.

▼ Four species of giant weta are at risk today. All are protected by law. They include the wetapunga, which has a soft body and sharp spines on its rear legs that it uses to defend itself.

Buried underground

Many insects spend most of their lives as caterpillars or larvae and have only very brief adult lives. However, the periodical cicadas of the United States and Canada take longer to mature than any other insects. Various species in the southeast spend 13 years buried underground as larvae. Others in the northeast take 17 years. When the cicadas do turn into adults, hundreds of thousands crawl out of the soil at once. They live only for a few weeks.

▲ This adult periodical cicada has just emerged from its chrysalis. While the cicada larvae are buried underground, their breeding sites may be built over or cleared for farming. It is very difficult to find and protect insects that are buried underground for so long.

Beetle survival

The world's longest beetle is the Hercules beetle. It measures up to 15 cm (6 in) in length and weighs about 15 g (0.5 oz).

There are several slight variations. One sub-species is found on the islands of Martinique and St. Lucia, and another on Dominica and Guadeloupe. These two particular types of Hercules beetles are classed as vulnerable. This means that they will soon become endangered unless steps are taken to protect them.

The threat to the Hercules beetles comes from the destruction of their habitat by tree-planters and farmers. The beetles are also being killed by the chemicals that are sprayed on the banana crops.

▼ Two male Hercules beetles fighting. The long "horns" of the male Hercules beetle take up over half its body length. Males may use their horns to fight rivals, but they rarely inflict an injury.

Sexton beetles

Sexton beetles feed on carrion, or dead animals. The beetles bury their food underground and then eat the rotting flesh. This may sound horrible, but the beetles perform a useful function. They help to clean up the forest floor and keep away flies and maggots. The soil is also fertilized by the beetles' activity.

The giant carrion beetle was once common, but during the 1960s and 1970s it was thought to have become extinct. However, a few have survived in New England. Huge areas of deciduous forest have been destroyed in North America. This loss of habitat is threatening the giant carrion beetle and many other insect species.

▼ The giant carrion beetle is black and red and measures up to 36 mm (1.4 in) long. It is the largest sexton beetle in North America.

Bees, wasps and ants

Hymenoptera is the name given by scientists to ants, bees, wasps, sawflies, gall wasps and ichneumons. These insects carry out useful jobs in the countryside. Bees carry pollen and so help plants and trees to bear fruit. Wasps eat aphids and caterpillars that would otherwise destroy many plants.

Over 50 Hymenoptera species, mostly in Europe and the United States, are under threat today. This is because chemicals sprayed on the crops destroy many insects. The mowing of grassy roadsides and the destruction of hedges are also a threat to bees and wasps. They need nesting sites, like old tree stumps and wooden gateposts, old walls, and bare sandy banks and footpaths, if they are to survive.

▼ One of the world's largest bees is found in the Moluccas, an island chain in Indonesia. Up to 39 mm (1.5 in) long, Wallace's giant bee was believed to be extinct until it was rediscovered in 1981. Although it has survived, its habitat is threatened by forest clearance and farming.

◄ Five species of wood ant are vulnerable in Europe. They vary in size from 6 to 11 mm (0.2 to 0.4 in) and are colored red, brown or black. Ants may bite and sting, but they also kill insect pests, help spread seeds and turn over the soil. These wood ants are collecting a sweet liquid called honeydew from aphids so that they can feed on it.

DID YOU KNOW?
- Ichneumons are commonly called flies, but they are in fact a kind of parasitic wasp. Parasitic wasps do not build nests for their young. Instead, they inject their eggs into the bodies of caterpillars or grubs of other wasps or bees after they have paralyzed them.
- Honey bees live in colonies of about 50,000 worker bees and 300 male bees, called drones. Each colony depends on a queen bee, who lays up to 2,000 eggs a day in spring.
- A large nest of wood ants can contain up to 300,000 workers. The workers live for one or two years, but the queens often live for 15.

INSECTICIDES
- The use of chemicals to kill insect pests can be reduced. Other insects can be introduced that will destroy the pests. For example, ladybugs can be released to kill aphids.

Insect action

It takes millions of years for animals to adapt and evolve. However, in the last few hundred years, the rate at which creatures have become extinct has increased dramatically. Thousands of insect species are disappearing before scientists have had the time to record their existence. The vast forests that once covered much of the earth's surface have been felled and burned. Crops have been sprayed with insecticides, killing the insects which eat the leaves or roots of the plants. Any insect that threatens humans is called a pest, and is destroyed.

By the year 2020, scientists think three million or more insect species may have become extinct as a result of human activity.

▼ A hundred years ago, collectors killed rare butterflies by the thousands. Some of the butterflies were put in glass cases and displayed like the collection below.

Today, rare species are protected by wildlife laws. Butterflies should be collected only for special scientific purposes.

This is serious enough for the insects, but it also matters for our own survival. Many of these creatures pollinate crops or control pests.

When a species of insect becomes extinct, it is too late to take action. When insects have disappeared in only part of their range, it is possible to breed them elsewhere and reintroduce them to their old habitat. The large blue butterfly became extinct in Britain in 1979. In 1984 and 1986, the butterfly was reintroduced into England from the Swedish island of Oland. More projects of this kind must be carried out all over the world for the conservation of wildlife.

▲ Butterfly farms help to inform the public about insect life and give people a rare chance to see butterflies at close quarters. Some farms help breed rare or endangered species for release into the wild.

Glossary

adapt To make suitable to new living conditions.

carrion The body of a dead animal eaten by another animal.

deciduous Shedding leaves each year.

endangered At risk of dying out.

entomology The scientific study of insects.

evolve To change with time. Creatures and plants evolve over millions of years as they adapt to changing living conditions.

extinct Disappeared, no longer living. Scientists now declare a creature to be officially extinct when it has not been seen in the wild for 50 years.

fossil The remains of ancient animals or plants preserved in rock.

habitat The place where an animal makes its home.

insecticide Any chemical used to kill insect life.

larva A stage in the life of an insect between egg and pupa or egg and adult.

nymph The young of an insect such as a dragonfly.

pest Any animal that is considered a nuisance to humans.

pollen The dusty powder carried by insects from one plant to another to produce fruit and seeds.

pupa A stage in the life of an insect between larva and adult.

range The geographical area in which an insect is found.

reintroduce To bring a species back to an area where it has died out.

resin A thick fluid produced by plants that, when hardened in the air, forms a hard, glassy substance. Fossils of insects are often found in hardened resin, like amber.

species A single group of identical animals or plants that can breed to produce like offspring.

vulnerable At risk of becoming endangered.

wetland A marshy or swampy habitat.

Find out more

- The study of insect life is called entomology. It can be a fascinating hobby. Just one oak tree is home to thousands of insects. Take a walk through woodlands or a park and look out for the many kinds of insects you will find there.

- Gardens provide ideal homes for insects. Many butterflies can be attracted to a garden if the right flowers and shrubs are planted. These include aubretia, honesty, lavender, and buddleia. A patch of unmown grass, nettles and dock leaves will provide food for many kinds of caterpillar.

- Many big cities have a museum of natural history or a science museum, where you can see fossilized insect remains and scientific collections which include insect species now extinct or endangered.

- Are you interested in helping to protect endangered insects around the world? The Wildlife Preservation Trust International sponsors the Dodo Club for young people. To find out more, write the Trust at 34th Street and Girard Avenue, Philadelphia, Pennsylvania 19104.

- Other addresses of interest:

  The National Wildlife Federation; 1412 16 Street, NW; Washington, DC 20036.

  American Entomological Society; 1900 Race Street; Philadelphia, PA 19103.

Time chart

<table>
<tr><td colspan="3">PREHISTORIC PERIOD</td></tr>
<tr><td>Years ago</td><td>Human history</td><td>Natural history</td></tr>
<tr><td>420–400 million</td><td></td><td>Scorpions, millipedes and early wingless insects evolve.</td></tr>
<tr><td>350 million</td><td></td><td>Winged insects such as cockroaches evolve.</td></tr>
<tr><td>310–290 million</td><td></td><td>Meganeura alive.</td></tr>
<tr><td>300 million</td><td></td><td>Rise of modern insect forms.</td></tr>
<tr><td>135 million</td><td></td><td>Evolution of flowering plants, fertilized by insects.</td></tr>
<tr><td>4 million</td><td>"Ape-people," such as Australopithecus, evolve.</td><td></td></tr>
<tr><td>100,000</td><td>Modern people evolve, hunters with weapons of stone. Gather insect grubs and the honey of wild bees for food.</td><td></td></tr>
<tr><td colspan="3">HISTORIC PERIOD</td></tr>
<tr><td>10,000-1500 B.C.</td><td>First farmers in Middle East. Chinese use ants to kill other insect pests – natural control. Silkworms (caterpillars) used to make silk in China. Beekeeping.</td><td>Changes in climate and vegetation.</td></tr>
<tr><td>1500 B.C.-A.D. 800</td><td>Classical period in Europe, followed by so-called Dark Ages. Greeks, Romans and ancient Chinese use sulfur and other naturally occurring chemicals as insecticides. Clearance of forests.</td><td>Loss of insect habitats.</td></tr>
<tr><td>800-1700</td><td>Widespread plagues in Asia and Europe carried by rat fleas. European settlement overseas.</td><td>Loss of insect habitats. Spread of plant species by travelers.</td></tr>
<tr><td>1700-1800</td><td>European settlement overseas. Beginnings of industry. Clearance of forests. Powdered tobacco used to kill aphids in France.</td><td>Loss of insect habitats.</td></tr>
<tr><td>1800-1900</td><td>European settlement overseas. Crop improvement. Use of lead arsenate as insecticide on farms. Butterfly collecting a popular hobby. Air and water pollution. Growth of interest in natural history and evolution.</td><td>Loss of insect habitats. Widespread insect destruction. Spread of insect predators such as rats, cats and poultry. Large copper butterfly extinct in Britain (1865).</td></tr>
<tr><td>1900-</td><td>Invention of DDT in Switzerland (1939). Deadly insecticide, now banned in many parts of the world. Destruction of rain forests and drainage of wetlands. Air and water pollution. Spraying of crops with insecticide from air. Spread of cities. Growth of interest in conservation and protection of environment.</td><td>Widespread destruction of disease-carrying or destructive insects, such as mosquitoes and locusts. Large blue butterfly extinct in Britain (1979). Lord Howe Island stick insect extinct (1980). Tobias Caddis fly extinct in Germany (1980). Use of insecticides poisons predatory bird species. The IUCN (1988) lists over 1,150 insect species as being at risk. These are all that are known. The actual figure is probably much higher.</td></tr>
</table>

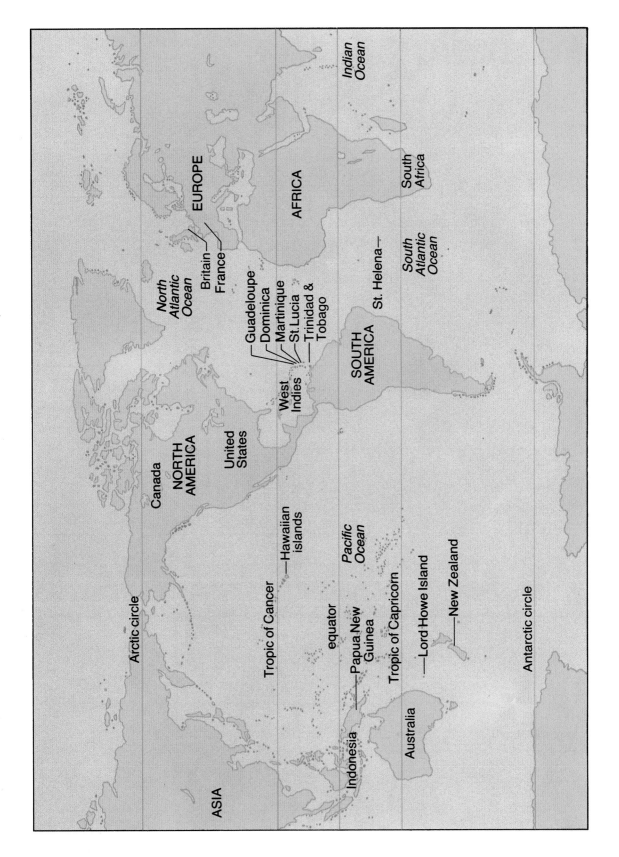

Arctic circle

North
Atlantic
Ocean

Canada

NORTH
AMERICA

United
States

EUROPE

Britain—
France

Guadeloupe
Dominica
Martinique
St. Lucia
Trinidad &
Tobago

West
Indies

AFRICA

South
Africa

St. Helena—

South
Atlantic
Ocean

SOUTH
AMERICA

Indian
Ocean

—Hawaiian
islands

Tropic of Cancer

Pacific
Ocean

equator

Papua New
Guinea

Tropic of Capricorn

—Lord Howe Island

—New Zealand

Antarctic circle

Indonesia

ASIA

Australia

31

Index